Aiming for Success

How to aim, build and stay at the top of your success.

While every precaution has been taken in the preparation of this book, the publisher assumes no responsibility for errors or omissions, or for damages resulting from the use of the information contained herein.

AIMING FOR SUCCESS

First edition. August 5, 2023.

ISBN: 979-8223375777

Written by Zondra dos Anjos.

"Success is the progressive realization of a worthy goal or ideal."

Earl Nightingale

5

Introduction

Climbing the ladder of success is no easy task, but with a little guidance and the right tools, it can be achieved. After years of research, I designed this book to provide you with the information and tools I used in my life, so you can make your way to the top and stay there permanently.

From understanding the basics of success to developing and implementing a plan to achieve it, this book will provide you with the necessary insight and guidance to help you ascend the ladder of success.

Working through the chapters, we will learn the essential steps to success, including going into the dept of your subconscious mind and changing it how you want. This book is not intended to provide you with a "quick fix" for success, but rather, it is designed to help you learn the skills and strategies necessary to achieve your version of success.

Along the way, we will also gain valuable insights into your own personal strengths and weaknesses, and how to leverage them to your advantage. I hope that this book will serve as a guide and a source of inspiration for you to reach your goals and climb the ladder of success.

Your Life, Your Rules.

Chapter 1 - Defined Goal

You may be wondering how to set a defined goal for yourself, this is the first step on your success ladder.

I'm here to tell you that it is possible to do so, and it doesn't have to be a difficult task.

In this chapter, I will share my experiences of setting a definite aim and how it has helped me reach my goals. I will also provide some tips and strategies that will help you create a successful definite aim for yourself.

Living a life without goals is like being a leaf in the wind.

I felt like that for many years and often asked myself why I couldn't achieve the success I wanted. My parents never taught me about success or money and goals. As I grew up, friends from school had a better life, and when I asked my parents, they answered in a way that made me understand that rich and successful people were evil and probably had money because they were taking advantage of someone.

Later on, I learned that living without a goal is the same as shouting to life, "I came to this world to do absolutely nothing." When you don't have a goal, procrastination, laziness, judgement, and sadness typically take its place, since without a direction, any direction is acceptable.

Deep in your heart, you have a burning desire to be successful – we all do. What you desire is already yours; Neville Goddard used to say,

"What you desire, desires you."

Living the life you want, doing what you like the most, meeting new people, expanding your business and network, traveling to the most exotic places on earth – this is the beautiful thing called life. And I didn't even mention money – because money is a consequence, not the journey – we will talk more about that later in this book.

Now I will share with you some essential topics, so you can set a Defined Goal exactly the way you want, with your own rules and in a way that you won't notice the changing of habits.

What do you want?

Decision-making is the main pillar of your Defined Goal. Sometimes it is difficult to decide because we are uncertain about the results. When you choose not to decide, it is also a decision.

What do you want in life? Money, to travel around the world, success, a good family, the love of your life, a good business, a good partnership? You can decide exactly what you want.

However, the Defined Goal requires you to stay true to your main decision and adjust it as needed. Without deciding what you want, how can you hope to achieve it?

Follow the plan.

Another important thing is to plan for what you have decided. In this plan, set a date, determine how you want to be by then, what you intend to have, and what you can use to help you along the way.

I often use the S.M.A.R.T. method for my goals; it's an easy way for me to keep track of my decisions and adjust them if I need to.

S.M.A.R.T. stands for:

Specific – What do you want to achieve?

Measurable – How will you know that you have achieved what you want?

Achievable – How can the goal be accomplished?

Realistic – Does this seem worthwhile?

Time-bound – When can I achieve this goal?

> Only by setting this plan systematically and sticking to it, you will
>
> create a starting point and keep yourself motivated along the way.

Directing your mind.

Now that you have decided and planned, it's time to direct your mind towards your Definite Goal.

Earl Nightingale frequently said, "We become what we think about most of the time.", our thoughts imprint our subconscious mind through repetition and autosuggestion.

In your daily life, think as frequently as possible about your goal and about what you can do today to take one more step in its direction.

Remember that thoughts create feelings that create behaviors and vice versa. Every day your mind will try to take you back to your old patterns of thoughts but be aware as much as possible so that you can use autosuggestion to give a new direction to your thoughts.

It's ok to fall back from time to time, so be present in the process and be kind to yourself for making this change.

Using the Definite Goal as a blueprint, Infinite Intelligence will

direct your mind towards what you want and will give you signs

through synchronicities along the way.

By following these steps, you will Define your Goal and bring it to pass.

Chapter 2 - Concentration

I'm glad you've picked up the plan lessons from the previous chapter and hope you are already planning on your dream goal. In this chapter, we are going to cover the second step on your success ladder; **Concentration.**

As an individual who has struggled with focus and concentration for much of my life, I understand the challenge of staying focused, especially when there are so many other distractions vying for our attention.

I will share some of my experiences and the strategies I have developed over the years to help me stay on track and make the most of my time. I am confident that you too can benefit from these techniques and achieve greater success in whatever you set your mind to.

Just One

Have you heard "one thing at the time" before? I had to hear that for many years to understand what I needed to do about it. You know when something has been shown to you or told you that is hard for you to take in?

It sounds simple, but it can be extremely hard. The world we live today is full of distractions and things that help to push you to be more distracted than ever. Distraction takes you away from your focus, your goals and also makes you forget things that are important to you.

To me, concentrating was difficult because I was used to multitasking, wanted to get things done fast, and you can imagine the results I got.

Many times the results were good, but other times not good at all because I understood afterward that where your focus is, there is also your results.

Focus on one thing at a time.

Mental Power

Concentration gathers all other mental faculties in an order way. Your perception, imagination, intuition, memory, will, and reason are enhanced when you keep your focus in place.

Those mental faculties are essential for the journey of building your ladder and staying permanently on your success path. Remember in the previous topic that I told you about distractions?

Well, the mobile phones, TVs, and all other distraction tools are designed to help you but also to affect your capacity to develop your mental faculties.

I had to learn how to awaken my faculties, and it's simpler than you can believe, if you have known my work, you also know that I am an advocate for the expansion of consciousness and believe that we are in full control of our mind, body, and spirit.

That there is no good and evil but free will, your choices can be your condemnation but also your victory and the communication that must happen on the inside.

Then I found out from a book by Florence Scovel Shinn a read once that calls "*The secret door to success*" that we can awaken the mental faculties by calling them.

For example: You get into a quiet state of mind and say: Intuition wake up, perception wake up and so on... and this worked like a magic for me.

- *Perception* is when you can solve situations, see people and understand things from a different perspective. When you are stuck in only one solution, call perception to help you, and you will start to see signs that point to other ways to see, understand and feel what you are going through.

- *Imagination* is your ability to create things before they come to pass, it's the Infinite Intelligence inside you, is like Dr. Joseph Murphy put on his lecture on imagination:

"It's the workshop of God".

In this mental faculty, **YOU ARE GOD**, and in your imagination you can be anywhere in a run of a second and omnipresent, you can build things, enjoy places.

None of this has to do with daydreaming but with using Divine Intelligence to plant into your subconscious mind what you want to happen. By the way, it works on the positive and negative perspectives.

Before you sleep, when you are in a drowsing state, that moment is where your conscious mind, also called as "The gatekeeper" gets out of the way, so your subconscious mind can be open for being sown.

At this moment, just before you sleep, imagine the life you want, see yourself talking with people about your success, be in the place, with the person, be there and build your dream life and then let your subconscious mind do the rest while you sleep and by automatically attracting to your life what you are designing.

An important point is to be aware because you will start to see synchronicities, signs, have ideas, insights about how and where is the next step in your journey.

- *Intuition* is the **GPS** of Divine Intelligence, is that calm voice that tells you "be careful with this" or "think through this".

This inner voice is there all times to prevent you from failing, is the Creator inside you guiding your path and soul mission in this life by living through you in His own creation.

- *Memory* says for itself, to remember things that are significant to your path and success. Often, people are afraid of remembering things because they link it to a hurtful experience, and then they link their mind, body and soul to it by avoiding it.

What you avoid working with gets bigger with time.

In my path, I had to use my memory to reframe all the hurt I had inside my heart and I learned that forgiveness does not equal reconnection.

Remembering that every time I remember something I read, learned, or heard, I can use it to help me or my clients.

Try to be aware every time you have a memory and ask your mental faculty: Memory, what is this for? What should I do with this? I am open for the Divine Intelligence inside me to guide my way. You can choose to talk to It in the way that is suitable for you.

- *Reason* is the mental faculty that makes you think cleverly, with the reason in place, you can make healthy decisions, keep yourself on track by making simple and small everyday choices that work in your favor.

You have probably heard people say "be reasonable" and it's easier said than done. When you are overwhelmed with issues, drama and negative situations, many times we want to think practically, but practicality is not always reasonable.

Nothing is done in a hurry.

In your everyday life, do what is more important that day, prioritize what is moving towards your success and be reasonable to say no to things that are not.

- ***Will*** is the mental faculty that makes things happen in your life. Bob Marley in his music Zion said, "If there is a will, there is always a way."

will is what opens the way and possibilities for you to achieve what you want.

When you are unmotivated and procrastinating it's easier to give up but try to call this mental faculty when this happens. ***Remember that will is your inner power.***

Choose

When you find what you want, make small daily choices and concentrate all your energy on this purpose until it reaches the best results.

It doesn't have to be perfect, but it has to be a result you are happy with.

Perfectionism is an illusion, so give yourself peace of mind by accepting that you did the best you could on your project. Celebrate yourself for what you have accomplished.

Chapter 3 - Self Control

Self-control is the ability to regulate one's thoughts, feelings, and behaviors. It is a fundamental skill that can be taught, practiced, and developed throughout life.

Self-control is essential for leading a healthy, successful, and fulfilling life. It is the key to making good decisions, managing stress, maintaining relationships, and achieving personal goals.

This chapter will provide the information and guidance you need to develop and maintain self-control.

Self-control is an essential skill that can have a positive impact on our lives. By developing and maintaining healthy self-control, we can achieve success, manage stress, and lead a more fulfilling life.

Masters

The person who has no self-control is mastered by the person who has it. When you don't have self-control, you are easily a target for feelings, thoughts, and people who want to take advantage of you.

By reacting to situations and circumstances you are giving your power to the external situation instead of being your powerful self.

Master yourself.

Emotions

When aiming to attain self-control, emotions are priority number one. If you master your emotions, nothing can harm you and if you master yourself, then you can achieve the limitless! You gain power by controlling your emotions.

Don't give anyone the privilege to control you. As Seneca states,

"Most powerful is he who has himself in his own power".

Suffering

Lack of self-control brings suffering, like I explained to you above, when you don't have self-control, you are most inclined to live your everyday life worrying about things that are outside your control and with that comes all the drama.

When you are in a mind state where outside circumstances decide how you are going to react, this is suffering. What is outside your control is none of your business.

Chapter 4 - Enthusiasm

In this chapter, I will be exploring the concept of enthusiasm and what it means to have a genuine and lasting passion for something. Enthusiasm can come in many forms and can take on different meanings depending on who you are.

We will be discussing the benefits of being enthusiastic, and how to create a more enthusiastic outlook on life. I believe that enthusiasm is essential in life, as it can make the difference between feeling fulfilled and achieving success or feeling bored and stuck in a rut.

This is why it is so important to be enthusiastic and to share it with others. By the end of this chapter, you will have a more profound understanding of the ***power of enthusiasm*** and that you have the tools to make it an integral part of your life.

The benefits

1- Being enthusiastic about something can bring a certain level of joy to life and make it easier to act towards achieving a goal. Having enthusiasm can also help us to stay motivated and passionate about what we are doing and can make it easier to overcome obstacles and reach our goals.

2- Furthermore, enthusiasm is contagious and when we are enthusiastic about something, we can inspire others to do the same. When we share this enthusiasm with others, it can be empowering and can create a sense of belonging and community.

3- Enthusiasm is a driving force that gives you a great power.

4- Enthusiasm gives power to your effort, by acting on what you want and having faith in the desired outcome.

5- Enthusiasm is a high vibrational energy for your mind.

6- Enthusiasm is the transmutation of sex drive force. By being enthusiastic, you use the most powerful energy in your body to achieve your goals.

7- The sex transmutation happens by changing the thought from sex contact to any other form of physical action.

When it comes to sexual force, many people can misinterpret what it really is and how it can be used in one's favor. This energy has the power to create life and that's why if a person, instead of releasing it in a meaningless way, use it with the power of desire to achieve a goal.

It's not about stopping your sex life, but with consciousness you will know how to distribute your energies in a much more effective way.

Chapter 5 - Profiting by Mistakes

We all make mistakes. Whether it's a small mistake like forgetting to turn off the lights or a bigger mistake like not studying for a test, mistakes are a part of life. But the good news is that mistakes can be fixed.

In this chapter, we'll explore how to give your mistakes another meaning, the importance of taking responsibility for our mistakes and how to do so in a constructive way, how to learn from our mistakes and use them to become better people, we'll also explore how to make amends and how to prevent similar mistakes in the future.

Finally, we'll look at how to move on from mistakes, the importance of forgiving ourselves and how to do so, you'll have a more profound understanding of how to profit from your mistakes.

You'll also have the tools and knowledge to take responsibility for your mistakes and move on from them in a constructive way. So, let's get started!

Overcoming mistakes

Giving mistakes another meaning and learning from them is an important part of growth. It is significant to remember that mistakes are not a sign of weakness but instead a sign of progress. Mistakes can be seen as opportunities to learn and grow.

One way to give mistakes another meaning is to take responsibility for them. Acknowledge the mistake and accept that it was your responsibility.

This can be difficult and uncomfortable, but it is necessary to move forward. Once you have taken responsibility for your mistake, it is essential to focus on the lessons that can be learned from it.

Consider what you could have done differently and how you could have avoided the mistake. This will help you to build self-awareness and develop strategies to avoid making the same mistake again.

Another way to give mistakes another meaning is to reframe them in a positive light. Instead of seeing the mistake as a failure, look at it as a chance to develop your skills.

Ask yourself what you can learn and how you can use the experience to your advantage. This will help you to take a more proactive approach and use the mistake as a platform to grow.

Practice self-compassion when making mistakes. Recognize that mistakes are part of the learning process. Be kind to yourself and take the time to reflect on the mistake. This will help you to move forward and create a more positive attitude towards mistakes.

Overall, mistakes can be seen as an opportunity to learn and grow. It is essential to take responsibility for your mistakes, reframe them in a positive light, and practice self-compassion. By doing so, you can give mistakes another meaning and learn from them.

Takeaways:

∞ Many people accept failure as permanent, don't be this kind of person.

∞ Failures are transitory, tales you from a place to another. It's all about perspective.

∞ Successful people must distinguish between failure and temporary defeat.

∞ Failure brings the best outcome.

∞ Life uses failure to show you that you are going the wrong direction, try again!

∞ The person who is afraid to fail don't allow themselves to see what needs to be corrected and improved in their life, so they can make decisions that are more aligned with their life purpose.

∞ Success meets adversity, failure, and temporary.

∞ What seems to be an unbearable obstacle, it is, until it has to be mastered.

∞ How you respond to adversity determines your success.

∞ Avoid being a "know all" and learn from your mistakes, people, and circumstances with humbleness. The person who "knows all" actually is insecure and this is their defending mechanism to don't take criticism.

Chapter 6 - Patience

Patience is one of the most essential virtues that we can develop in life. It is a quality that allows us to remain calm and composed in the face of adversity, to persevere through difficult situations, and to maintain a positive attitude in the midst of uncertainty.

In this chapter, we will explore the origin of the word "patience," the benefits and advantages of being patient, and how we can cultivate this valuable trait in our lives.

The Origin

The word "patience" comes from the Latin word "pati," which means "to suffer" or "to endure." The original meaning of the word was not simply to wait calmly for something to happen, but to endure hardship and suffering with fortitude and courage.

In this sense, patience was seen as a strength rather than a weakness, a quality that enabled people to withstand the trials of life and emerge stronger and wiser as a result.

Today, the meaning of the word has evolved somewhat, but the essence of patience remains the same.

Being patient means having the ability to wait calmly and without complaint, to remain steadfast in the face of obstacles and setbacks, and to persevere in the pursuit of our goals despite the challenges that we may encounter along the way.

The benefits

So, what are the benefits of being patient?

First, patience allows us to stay focused and committed to our long-term goals. When we are patient, we can resist the temptation to give up or to take shortcuts, and we are more likely to achieve success in the end.

Patience also makes us more resilient and adaptable, allowing us to weather the storms of life with grace and equanimity.

In addition to these benefits, there are many advantages to being patient. For one thing, patience can strengthen our relationships with others. When we are patient, we are better able to listen to and understand the perspectives of others, and we are less likely to become defensive or argumentative.

This can make us more empathetic, more compassionate, and more effective at building strong and meaningful relationships with those around us.

Another advantage of patience is that it can improve our overall wellbeing. When we are patient, we are more likely to experience feelings of peace, contentment, and satisfaction.

We are less likely to feel stressed, anxious, or overwhelmed, and we are more able to enjoy life's simple pleasures and joys. This can lead to a greater sense of happiness and fulfillment, and can help us to live more fully and joyfully in the present moment.

Chapter 7 - Accurate Thinking

We are often faced with situations that require us to think critically and make decisions based on the available information. However, not all of us possess the ability to think accurately and make informed choices. This is where accurate thinking comes into play.

Accurate thinking is the practice of examining and evaluating information in a systematic and methodical manner. It enables us to make rational decisions by analyzing the facts and considering different perspectives.

Accurate thinking also helps us identify biases and assumptions that may influence our decision-making process, allowing us to make more objective choices.

In this chapter, we will delve deeper into the concept of accurate thinking and explore its importance in our daily lives. We will examine some common pitfalls that can lead to inaccurate thinking and provide practical strategies for developing this critical skill.

So, whether you are a student, a professional, or simply someone looking to improve your decision-making abilities, this chapter is for you. Let's begin the journey towards accurate thinking!

The Facts

Accurate thinking is a vital skill that enables us to differentiate between facts and information that may not be relevant. It is essential to learn how to separate the two. One way to do this is by dividing the facts into two categories, Important and Irrelevant.

An important fact is one that aligns with your goals or relates to your profession and can be useful in helping you achieve your objectives. As you work towards achieving your goals, it is crucial to avoid engaging in conversations that do not have any factual basis.

Success is an outcome of a combination of factors such as perseverance, self-sacrifice, determination, and strong character. All these attributes require accurate thinking.

Accurate thinking demands effort, and it involves gathering and organizing facts upon which we base our thoughts. The ability to identify and arrange information systematically is critical in ensuring that our thoughts are not misguided and lead us towards our goals effectively.

It is evident that accurate thinking is essential for success. It is an art that requires patience, discipline, and practice. The importance of accurate thinking lies in its ability to help us remain focused on our goals.

By separating important facts from irrelevant ones, we become more efficient in our decision-making processes. We can make informed choices, knowing that our decisions are based on relevant information.

When we approach situations with accurate thinking, we can analyze them objectively. We can identify both the opportunities and challenges that they present. This approach allows us to address issues proactively and take advantage of the opportunities presented. Inaccurate thinking may lead us to miss opportunities or fail to address issues that require our attention.

Accurate thinking is an essential component of success.

It enables us to distinguish between facts and irrelevant information, allowing us to make informed decisions. Accurate thinking requires effort and discipline, but it is an art that can be mastered through practice.

With accurate thinking, we can achieve our goals, acquire new skills, and be successful in our personal and professional lives.

Chapter 8 - Fertile Subconscious

Have you ever found yourself lost in a daydream, your mind wandering to places beyond your physical surroundings? Perhaps you've envisioned new worlds filled with fantastical creatures or imagined yourself as the hero in a daring adventure.

These types of imaginative experiences are not only enjoyable, but they can also be surprisingly beneficial for our mental health and creativity.

The concept of an imagination fertile subconscious is rooted in the idea that our minds are not limited by our present reality and that our subconscious can offer us a wealth of unique and creative ideas.

When we tap into our subconscious mind through creative activities such as writing, drawing, or daydreaming, we allow ourselves to explore uncharted territories and unleash untapped potential.

Let's dive into the idea of an fertile subconscious, exploring its benefits and how we can access it more effectively. You will understand the power of your imagination and how to harness its potential to enrich your life and enhance your creativity.

The divine work space.

Imagination is one of the most powerful mental faculties that we possess. It is the ability to create mental images, concepts, and ideas that are not immediately present in our physical reality. It is the driving force that shapes our dreams, ambitions, and projects.

Without imagination, human beings would not have been able to create anything new, innovative or meaningful.

The power of imagination can be seen in various fields, including arts, science, technology, and literature. For example, when an artist creates a painting, they first imagine the image in their mind before they put it on canvas.

When a scientist formulates a hypothesis, they imagine the results of their experiments. Similarly, when a writer writes a novel, they imagine the characters, plot, and setting before putting pen to paper.

Imagination also helps us to solve problems and find new ways of doing things. We can use our imaginations to visualize different scenarios and outcomes, which allows us to make better decisions.

Imagination is essential for innovation and progress as it enables us to think outside the box and come up with creative solutions to complex problems.

Takeaways

∞ Collect every idea, thought, and work them into a new plan.

∞ The imagination will suggest ideas because it will pick up information from the subconscious mind.

∞ Imagination is important to gather knowledge because the subconscious mind is filled with them.

∞ Put your insights into action.

∞ Imagination is a mental faculty that provides us with the creativity and inspiration needed to shape our dreams, ambitions, and projects.

∞ It is a driving force that helps us to overcome obstacles, make better decisions and solve problems. Cultivate and nurture your imagination by exposing ourselves to diverse experiences, ideas, and perspectives.

Chapter 9 - Genius Mind

A genius mind can see beyond the limits of conventional wisdom, to unearth new ideas, and to identify solutions to complex problems. It can transcend boundaries and bring about a paradigm shift in the way we perceive the world around us.

With their unique perspectives and creative insights, geniuses have the power to challenge the status quo, push boundaries, and inspire others to think differently.

The power of a genius mind is not just limited to academia and the arts, but it also has practical applications in everyday life. From inventors like Thomas Edison to entrepreneurs like Steve Jobs, geniuses have left an indelible mark on the business world, revolutionizing industries, and creating new ones.

By gaining a deeper understanding of the genius mind, we can unlock our potential and achieve greatness in our fields of endeavor.

Intense Desire

One of the main factors to having a genius mind is the desire to attain this state of mind. Knowledge is never too much for a genius and once you start to search for knowledge you get hungrier for it.

Everything becomes a trigger for intelligent curiosity, you start to read and do research on subjects you once never thought you would, you open your mind to learn every day, you open yourself for new theories and goals that once, in your understanding would have been impossible for you to attain.

Desire is the fuel of success and wish is a passive form of desire.

Stimulating Points

There are seven stimulating points to activate the genius mind and intense desire.

1- The urge of self-preservation.

When we are in survival mode, we prioritize the essentials of our daily living. We work diligently each day to improve our life circumstances or simply sustain the ones we have. If we already possess all that we desire, we strive to consistently perform at our personal best.

2- Desire for sexual contact.

Sex is a natural and fundamental aspect of human life and existence. It is the energy that creates new life and serves as a means of expressing our deepest desires and passions. Through sexual intimacy, we experience a release of energy and emotion, allowing us to connect with our partners on a deeper level.

Sex provides us with the strength and vitality necessary to pursue our goals and aspirations, ensuring personal growth and fulfillment. By embracing our sexual nature and desires, we can tap into a powerful source of energy that drives us towards happiness and success.

3- Desire for financial gains.

The desire for financial gains can be a powerful motivator that impels people to act and pursue their goals with zeal and determination. The allure of wealth and prosperity can be hard to resist, as it offers a means of attaining security, comfort, and independence.

Many people dream of financial success, hoping to achieve it through hard work, perseverance, and savvy decision-making. While the pursuit of wealth can be rewarding and fulfilling, it can also be fraught with challenges and pitfalls.

It's important to have a clear sense of priorities and values before setting out on a quest for financial gain, ensuring that your goals are aligned with your moral compass and long-term aspirations.

4- Desire for fame to possess power.

The desire for fame and power is an urge that has captivated people since the beginning of civilization. The thirst for recognition, attention, and control can be a driving force in shaping one's aspirations and worldview.

Many people seek to make a name for themselves, hoping to leave a legacy that will be remembered long after they're gone. Power can be seductive, as it offers individuals the ability to influence and shape the world around them with their words and actions.

The pursuit of fame and power can also be dangerous, as it can lead to arrogance, greed, and corruption. It's important to be mindful and cautious when seeking these things, making sure that our desires are grounded in a sense of purpose and a desire to serve others.

5- Urge for love, separate and distinct from sex urge.

The urge for love is an innate and powerful desire that is separate and distinct from the urge for sex. The need to bond, connect and feel accepted by others is a fundamental aspect of human experience. From birth, we seek connection with other people and often form bonds that last a lifetime.

A genuine connection with another person can bring great joy and fulfillment to our lives, nourishing us on an emotional and psychological level. The desire for love can be intense, often driving us to take risks and make changes in our lives to find it.

Differentiating the urge for love from the desire for sex, can be easily confusing.

Love involves a deep emotional connection with another person, while sex is a physical act that can exist independently of love. By recognizing the difference between the two urges, we can approach our relationships with greater clarity and understanding, forming deeper connections with those around us.

6- Desire for revenge

The desire for revenge is a primal and often overwhelming urge that can be prevalent in the more undeveloped minds.

When we feel wronged or hurt by another person, the desire for payback can be incredibly strong, driving us to seek some form of retribution. It's a natural human response to want to right a perceived wrong, and the desire for revenge can often feel empowering.

Often, the desire for revenge can be harmful, both to the person seeking it and to others around them. It's important to recognize that revenge doesn't always bring closure or satisfaction and often leads to a cycle of violence and negativity.

To move past the desire for revenge, it's crucial to process our emotions and work towards forgiveness and moving forwards. By doing so, we can break the cycle of retaliation and create a healthier and more positive future for ourselves and those around us.

7- Desire to indulge one's egotism.

The desire to indulge one's egotism is a complex and often self-destructive behavior that can lead to a wide range of negative outcomes. Egotism refers to an excessive focus on oneself, often at the expense of others.

Characterized by a belief that one is superior to others and deserves special treatment.

The desire to indulge one's egotism can result in an over-inflated sense of self-importance, leading to arrogance and an inability to accept constructive criticism. This can seriously damage relationships and limit social interaction.

On the other hand, indulging in one's egotism can also bring temporary pleasure and satisfaction, as it validates one's sense of self-worth. However, such pleasure is often short-lived, as it rarely brings genuine fulfillment or happiness. Striving for humbleness and focusing on the needs of others around you can lead to a more fulfilling and meaningful life, free from the negative consequences of egotism.

Takeaways

∞ Harmony is an important element in a genius mind.

∞ The intense desire for sexual contact produces creativity, ideas, inspiration, and revelation. The redirection of sexual energy is named as sexual transmutation.

∞ An attractive person is a person who has a genius mind active. This attraction doesn't have anything to do with how one looks.

∞ The mind that is constantly active towards a purpose gets impulses and ideas from inspirations and revelations.

Other stimulants (positive and negative)

- Love.
- Music.
- Friendship.

- Mastermind alliances.
- Auto-suggestion.
- Suggestion from outside.
- Narcotics and alcohol.

Those stimuli put the mind in contact with Infinite Intelligence even if negatively, that might result in suffering and not the attainment of desired success. You must remember that it's all about choices, and you are the only one who is responsible for yourself.

Chapter 10 - Save = Multiply

It is a common saying that 'money begets money,' and this statement holds a lot of truth in the world of finances. It is not enough to earn money; what you do with your earnings will determine how much it will grow in the future.

One of the essential practices for multiplying wealth is saving. Saving can be difficult, especially if you have a limited budget or many financial commitments. However, the secret to successful saving is to make it a habit.

> By consistently putting aside a portion of your earnings, however small,

> you can gradually build up your savings and pave the way to financial security.

In the book Rules Of Wealth By Richard Templar, says that money goes for who have money and this is very truth because like attracts like, take the water as an example. The water from your residence, after undergoing a prolonged process, is subsequently transported to rivers, lakes, or the sea. So, water goes back to the water.

Some advantages of saving:

1. It helps in emergencies

Emergencies are always unexpected. Therefore, when they occur, the funds required are usually not part of your regular budget. There is often pressure to look for extra funds at a very short notice, such as funeral expenses, house repairs and even car repairs. Accumulated savings can often go a long way in alleviating these emergencies.

2. Cushions against sudden job loss

You may have a good job now, but what if (God forbid) you were to lose that job? Suddenly finding yourself unemployed can be frightening and traumatic, but it's something many people will experience at some point in their lives. Having savings in place to help cover your living expenses while you find a new job can provide you with peace of mind.

3. Helps finance those big-ticket items and major life events

Whether you're looking to buy a house or car, tie the knot or even start a family, many big life events can often carry a hefty price tag. For some of these the thought of reaching for a credit card or taking out a personal loan is all too easy.

However, using savings to help fund these things is a much better option than putting yourself in debt and having to repay the funds borrowed along with interest. Some of these, such as purchasing a property, doesn't allow for borrowed funds to be used anyway, so the money required will need to have been saved regardless.

4. Limits debt

Having some amount in savings can help to limit the amount of debt needed, as they can be used to finance certain expenses instead of using a credit card or personal loan. This will limit the request of further funds and will also allow you to save the amount that would have been spent on interest.

Savings also help avoid the need to take out emergency loans when urgent situations occur, which often come with a higher interest rate.

5. Helps prepare for retirement

When you start the savings habit, it pays to think about the long term, as well as what might be just around the corner. The state pension itself is unlikely to provide you with enough income to cover all your costs when you eventually stop work, particularly as the age at which you'll be able to claim it is moving gradually further away, so the earlier you think about retirement planning the better.

Making a habit of saving a small portion of your income over several years can accumulate into a substantial amount of retirement funds, which will help to make your retirement much more comfortable.

Chapter 11 - Abundance as a habit

Abundance can be defined as having more than enough of what you need in your life. It is a state of mind where you feel grateful and fulfilled, and where you can attract and manifest positive outcomes.

> Having abundance as a habit is about cultivating a mindset and
>
> lifestyle that supports this state of being.

It's about recognizing the abundance that already exists in your life, and practicing habits that help you attract more of it. In this chapter, we will explore several key habits that can help you develop an abundance mentality and improve your overall sense of well-being.

From gratitude and generosity to visualization and self-care, these habits will help you cultivate a mindset of abundance and transform your life for the better. Abundance is often associated with material wealth and possessions.

Abundance is much more than just having an excess of material things. It is a state of mind that can be cultivated as a habit. When abundance becomes a habit, it affects every aspect of our lives.

It enables us to approach challenges with a positive attitude, to focus on solutions rather than problems, and to see opportunities where others see obstacles.

An abundant mindset also allows us to appreciate the simple pleasures in life and be grateful for what we have. Abundance can be developed as a habit and can transform our lives for the better.

How to attract abundancy daily:

∞ Avoid discussing the lack of resources.

∞ Make sure to focus on the good things in your life.

∞ Avoid walking with people who live in a scarcity mindset.

∞ Get out of your comfort zone every day.

∞ Feel blessed in all your endeavors.

∞ Let go of what made you feel bad.

∞ Avoid interacting with people who are harmful to you.

∞ Don't engage in a complaining behavior.

∞ Be grateful for the good and the bad situations.

∞ Avoid the blame game.

∞ Don't feel sorry for yourself, get out of victimization.

∞ What happened made you stronger.

Chapter 12 - Irresistible Personality

Having an irresistible personality is a power.

Have you ever met someone who just radiates positive energy, charm, and charisma? Someone whose mere presence commands attention and respect, someone who seems to effortlessly connect with others and leave a lasting impression? If so, you have experienced the power of an irresistible personality.

An irresistible personality is more than just physical attractiveness or social skills—it goes deeper than that. It is rooted in a combination of inner qualities and outer behaviors that together create a magnetic presence that draws people in.

Whether we are aware of it or not, we are all constantly evaluating those around us based on their personality traits and behaviors, and when we encounter someone with an irresistible personality, we are naturally drawn to them.

Let's explore the key traits and behaviors of an irresistible personality, learn how to cultivate them in ourselves and examine the ways in which an irresistible personality can boost your personal and professional lives, from building stronger relationships to advancing our careers.

Creating an irresistible personality.

Here are some ideas for you to align your personality and make your personality irresistible. Based on successful people, those are the traits of a successful person:

∞ Curiosity – Always try to find out more about things.

∞ Versatile – Do many things well.

∞ Creative – Know how to put things together.

∞ Drive – Desire to work hard and long towards what you want.

∞ Courage – Perseverance of purpose, you do what you have to do even if it's scary.

∞ Goals – You know what you want, and you take small steps every day.

∞ Knowledge – You want to know more and more about your interests. You have an insatiable thirst for knowledge and always want to learn more.

∞ Health – You praise your health by eating good food, enjoying eating what you like without guilt, you move your body because you know it's good for you.

∞ Optimism – You believe in yourself and you are part of a solution to a problem and not part of the problem.

∞ Enthusiasm – You want success for yourself and for others.

∞ Honesty – You know that honesty gives you a good night sleep and less to think about.

∞ Judgement – You understand and then judges.

∞ Chance Taker – You take chances because you know life is too short to live in fear.

∞ Inventive – You take opportunities, and you are not afraid of the unknown.

∞ Outgoing – You make good friends and people around you grow.

∞ Dynamic – You are energetic and want more.

∞ Persuasive – You know how to sell and how to talk to people on different levels.

∞ Patient – You know that what has to be yours comes to you and that's why you wait for the best opportunities.

∞ Sensitive – You are in the present as often as you can.

∞ Flexible – You have an open mind to hear other people theories and learn more.

∞ Humor – You laugh of silly things and make enjoyable jokes.

We all make mistakes; your mistakes do not determine your future. If right now you don't have any of those above, make small changes every single day.

Each day should be an opportunity and adventure to overcome your old habits, and you will soon see that you have achieved what you want. Success is not something that comes easy, you must insist, and sometimes it can take years for you to achieve what you want. You will fall in love with the process and when this happens, you live life as it should be lived.

Chapter 13 - Leader's Initiative

Leadership is often attributed to an individual's ability to take charge and make decisions. True leadership goes beyond just directing others, it involves demonstrating initiative. An initiative is an action taken to solve a problem or improve a situation without being asked or directed.

A leader who takes the initiative can set a positive tone for their team and inspire others to follow their lead. A leader who demonstrates initiative shows that they are not afraid to take risks, think creatively, and take ownership of their actions.

Leaders and Followers

Not everyone is born to be a leader, for many people that's totally fine to be a follower, they feel they get more inspired by their mentors and see in them an example of life.

Be content with the place life has given you, be grateful, always give your best, if you have a burning desire to be a leader, and it's in your destiny, don't worry you will, but if not, do you best where you are.

Paid Skills

A man is paid for what he knows and what he makes others do. If you have skills and those skills might help other people, most people will pay you gladly to teach them what you know.

There is a history of The Ivy Lee method dated back to 1918, when Lee, a productivity consultant, was hired by Charles M. Schwab, the president of the Bethlehem Steel Corporation, to improve his company's efficiency. As the story goes, Lee offered his method to Schwab for free, and after three months, Schwab was so pleased with the results he wrote Lee a check for $25,000 — the equivalent of about $400,000 today.

The Ivy Lee method is to write down the six most important things you have to do the next day and number them by importance and priority.

In the next day, start with the most important and move on to the next only when you are done. This will keep you focused and make you work on your tasks more efficiently.

Educate yourself and find out what type of intelligence you have in the list below. When you use what you have best, you leverage your productivity and marked value.

The eight types of intelligence – Find out yours.

Logical-mathematical intelligence

Your problem-solving ability is very striking and is often related to a type of non-verbal intelligence, i.e., you can know the answer to a certain problem long before you verbalize it.

As a child, you may have been good at solving mysteries or brain-teasers, doing puzzles, logic exercises, counting or doing calculations, computer problems, and playing strategy games, which are indicative of your type of intelligence.

Linguistic intelligence

If you possess this type of intelligence, you are likely skilled and have preferences for activities such as reading, talking, telling stories and jokes, writing poems, learning languages, and playing word games.

Spatial Intelligence

If you possess this type of intelligence, you are likely skilled in thinking in three dimensions and can solve spatial problems such as drawing and painting, reading maps, looking at pictures, solving mazes, or playing construction games.

Musical Intelligence

It is typical of children with an innate ability to learn different sounds, which translates into a great ability to sing, listen to music, play instruments, compose songs, enjoy concerts, and follow different rhythms. This type of intelligence may notice off-key notes that others do not and can easily memorize songs and tunes.

Bodily kinesthetic Intelligence

If you possess kinesthetic intelligence, you can use your whole body in the expression of ideas and feelings and are skilled in the use of your hands to transform elements. As a child, you may have been good at activities such as dancing, acting, imitating gestures or expressions, playing sports, running, moving, and jumping.

Intrapersonal Intelligence

If you possess this trait, you are likely someone who knows yourself best. You prefer to work independently, set goals, and focus on achieving them, and you understand your feelings as well as your strengths and weaknesses.

Interpersonal Intelligence

If you do not possess intrapersonal intelligence, it is common for you to excel in social situations such as talking, working in teams, helping others, mediating conflicts, and meeting new people.

Naturalistic intelligence

If you possess this type of intelligence, you likely have an attraction towards environmental issues, plants, and animals. You may enjoy doing activities such as camping, hiking, caring for animals, learning about nature, recycling, and caring for the environment.

Leaders who take initiative are essential for any successful organization or team. By being proactive and taking charge, they set an example for others to follow and can identify new opportunities for growth and improvement.

> Effective leaders with initiative are not afraid to take risks and can inspire
>
> their team members to greater levels of productivity and achievement.

By cultivating initiative, organizations can create an environment where ideas are freely shared, innovation thrives, and success is inevitable. Therefore, leadership with initiative is an indispensable quality that every leader should strive to embody and cultivate.

Chapter 14 - Partnership

Partnership is a concept that has been integral to human society since the beginning of civilization. It is a relationship that involves two or more individuals or entities coming together for a common purpose.

Partnerships can take various forms, such as business partnerships, strategic alliances, joint ventures, and even personal partnerships.

At its core, partnership is about cooperation, collaboration, and mutual trust. It offers an opportunity for individuals or entities to combine their strengths, resources, and expertise to achieve greater success than they could alone. Effective partnerships can result in innovative solutions, improved performance, increased efficiency, and ultimately, better outcomes.

Cooperation

It's crucial for you to gain the cooperation of others in a partnership. If you don't have people in your life who are willing to cooperate with you, it may be because you are not surrounding yourself with the right people, or you don't have the right attitude towards them.

You need to reflect on your behavior and judge whether any changes need to be made. Having people who support you and can help you when you need it makes it easier for you to achieve success at a faster pace.

Avoid being arrogant, make your points in a humble manner and be willing to move on to the next topic when discussing things.

Collaboration

Collaboration is an essential aspect of any partnership. When two or more people work together towards a common goal, they bring unique skills, expertise, and perspectives to the table.

Through collaboration, partners can share ideas, support and motivate each other, and create a more effective and cohesive team. Effective collaboration requires trust, communication, and a willingness to compromise and work towards the overall success of the partnership.

Trust

Trust plays a crucial role in any partnership. For you to build a strong partnership, you need to have faith in your partner or team abilities, beliefs, and decisions.

It's important to communicate openly, honestly, and transparently with each other and avoid keeping secrets or hiding information that can cause doubts. Mutual trust enables you to work together towards your common goals, take risks, and support each other through the ups and downs of the partnership.

Remember that working with others is a journey, not a destination. It takes time, effort, and a willingness to learn and adapt to each other's strengths and weaknesses. Remember to focus on building trust, communicating effectively, and collaborating towards your common goals.

With the right mindset, attitude, and approach, you can create a successful and enriching partnership and team that benefits everyone involved. Keep pushing forward and never lose sight of your vision.

Chapter 15 - Getting more with less effort.

In today's fast-paced world, where time is a luxury and productivity is the key to success, people are always looking for ways to get more done in less time. Whether it's at work or at home, we all want to achieve our goals and ambitions without having to put in too much effort.

But is it really possible to get more with less effort? Can we truly be productive without sacrificing our well-being and sense of balance?

The answer is yes, and in this chapter, we will explore some strategies that can help you maximize your output and minimize your workload. So, if you're ready to learn how to work smarter, not harder, then keep reading and discover how you can get more done with less effort.

Pomodoro Technique

The technique consists of breaking down work into short, 25-minute intervals called "Pomodoros," separated by five-minute breaks. After four consecutive Pomodoros, a longer break of 15–20 minutes is taken.

This technique aims to improve concentration and productivity by allowing regular breaks and preventing burnout. Additionally, it encourages individuals to focus on one task at a time, minimizing distractions and increasing efficiency.

Kaizen

A philosophy of continuous improvement, focusing on making small, incremental changes to processes and systems. Today better than yesterday and tomorrow better than today.

5S

A systematic method for organizing and maintaining a clean, efficient workspace, consisting of five principles: Sort, Set in Order, Shine, Standardize, and Sustain. When you have an organized workspace, things flow easily.

The 80/20 Rule (Pareto Principle)

The idea that 80% of results come from 20% of efforts, can help identify and prioritize important tasks. Focus on what is important for you.

Single Tasking

Focusing on one task at a time, rather than multitasking, to increase efficiency and reduce distractions.

Mind Mapping

A visual tool for organizing and brainstorming ideas, typically represented as a diagram with branches emanating from a central concept.

GTD (Getting Things Done)

A time management method that emphasizes the importance of organizing tasks and maintaining a clear to-do list.

Now that you have some techniques to increase your workflow, start today by using the technique you resonate better with.

Chapter 16 - Success and its ways

Success is a term that has been defined and redefined time and again. It may mean different things to different people, and the ways to achieve it can vary greatly depending on who you ask.

One thing is for certain: most of us strive to attain some

level of success in our lives.

Whether it's in our personal relationships, career, finances, or other aspects of our lives, we all want to experience a sense of accomplishment and fulfillment.

The concept of success

The concept of success varies from person to person. For some, success may mean achieving financial stability, while for others, success may involve becoming a renowned artist or athlete.

Success is achieved when an individual has fulfilled their personal goals and aspirations.

Success can be achieved through a combination of hard work, dedication, perseverance, and focus. It's important to note, however, that success is not a finite destination, but rather a continuous journey in which all individuals can continually strive towards.

Success can be immensely rewarding, but it's significant to define success in a way that's meaningful to you personally, and not base it on societal standards or other external factors.

Determining Success

Factors such as upbringing, education, natural talent, hard work, perseverance, and mindset can all play a role in an individual's success. However, what may work for one person may not work for another since everyone has different cultural contexts, values, and beliefs.

Some individuals may place a higher emphasis on financial gain and economic stability, while others may prioritize personal fulfillment and happiness. At the end of the day, success is unique and personal to everyone, and people define it according to their aspirations, desires and goals.

Don't compare your success journey with someone else's because each

individual has different strengths and challenges they're dealing with.

Chapter 17 - Mastering Success

Mastering success is a skill that is sought after by people from all walks of life. Whether you are an ambitious student, an aspiring entrepreneur, or a seasoned professional, the ability to achieve success can lead to a fulfilling and rewarding life.

Success is not an overnight achievement, it takes time, dedication, and perseverance to reach one's goals.

Ingredients to success

The ingredients to success can vary depending on the context, but here are some.

Confidence: Self-confidence is considered a crucial ingredient for success. Having belief in oneself and one's abilities can help overcome challenges and take risks.

Self-Awareness: Understanding oneself, including strengths, weaknesses, values, and goals, is important for setting the right path and making informed decisions.

Self-Belief: Believing in one's potential and abilities is essential for staying motivated and determined even in the face of obstacles.

Self-Discipline: Developing self-discipline involves cultivating habits and routines that contribute to productivity, focus, and consistent effort towards goals.

Self-Motivation: Success often requires a strong internal drive to keep going, persevere, and maintain motivation despite setbacks.

Patience: Success may take time, and being patient allows one to stay committed and persist even when results are not immediate.

Setting Goals: Clearly defining and setting goals is significant for directing efforts and measuring progress.

Hard Work and Effort: Success generally requires consistent and dedicated effort towards achieving goals.

Learning and Growth: Continuous learning, adaptability, and a willingness to improve are important for staying relevant and excelling in a changing environment.

Resilience: Success often involves overcoming challenges and setbacks, and being resilient helps bounce back and keep moving forward.

Note that success is a subjective concept and can be defined differently for each individual or situation. These ingredients can serve as general guidelines, but it's important to tailor them to personal circumstances and priorities.

Always Learning

Learning from failure and using setbacks as opportunities for growth are integral aspects of personal and professional development. Failure, rather than being an endpoint, should be embraced as a steppingstone towards success.

When we encounter setbacks, we have the chance to reflect, adapt, and learn valuable lessons that can propel us forward. By analyzing what went wrong, we gain insights into areas that require improvement. It allows us to reassess our strategies, approaches, and perspectives, fostering creativity and innovation.

> Embracing failure teaches us resilience, as we understand that setbacks are not permanent roadblocks but temporary hurdles that can be overcome. Failure provides us with invaluable opportunities for self-discovery and growth. It enables us to

understand our limits, uncover hidden strengths, and develop new skills. By embracing failure and using setbacks as stepping stones, we can transform obstacles into opportunities and continue on the path towards success.

Chapter 18 - Golden Rules

In the quest for success in life, there are several golden rules that have stood the test of time. These rules are tried and tested principles that have been proven to lead to success in various aspects of life – from personal relationships to career advancement.

They are simple yet powerful, and when applied consistently, they can make an enormous difference in one's life. In this chapter, we will explore these golden rules of success and how you can apply them to your life to achieve success.

Whether you are just starting out on your journey in life or looking for ways to enhance your current success, these golden rules will provide you with practical tips and advice that can help you make the most of your potential and achieve the success you deserve.

1st. Law—What you do is done unto you.

This is the Universal Law of Action/Reaction, it's simple; what you do is done to you regardless if you are right or wrong.

2nd. Law—Like attracts like.

It doesn't help to desire success if you are not successful, you don't need money to start, don't need to come from a wealthy family. The only thing you need is to make a list of what you want to attract and be the things from the list.

For example: You wish to attract a good relationship, you can start taking care of yourself, being faithful to yourself, keeping the promises to yourself and giving yourself love by not putting yourself into difficult situations or dealing with toxic people.

3rd. Law – Law of Exchange.

There is no take without giving. If you are taking, somehow the Universe will take from you.

If you give, the Universe will also give you.

For example: You are dependent emotionally, insecure and want attention. You want someone's attention; you are insisting on taking their time and so on.

The Universe will find a way to put someone in your way to also take your energy and time, and if it is not thought another human being, it will be thought yourself or if you render a service to someone and the person doesn't give/respond back, the Universe will find a way to give you back what you put out.

"What you sow, shall you reap".

Don't miss out!

Visit the website below and you can sign up to receive emails whenever Zondra dos Anjos publishes a new book. There's no charge and no obligation.

https://books2read.com/r/B-A-RTVZ-KZNMC

BOOKS 2 READ

Connecting independent readers to independent writers.

Also by Zondra dos Anjos

Demystifying the Tarot - The 22 Major Arcana.
Demystifying the Tarot - The Fool
Demystifying the Tarot - The Magician
Demystifying the Tarot - The High Priestess
Demystifying the Tarot - The Empress
Demystifying the Tarot - The Emperor
Demystifying the Tarot - The Hierophant
Demystifying the Tarot - The Lovers
Demystifying the Tarot - The Chariot
Demystifying the Tarot - The Strength
Demystifying the Tarot - The Hermit
Demystifying the Tarot - The Wheel of Fortune
Demystifying the Tarot - Justice
Demystifying the Tarot - The Hanged Man
Demystifying the Tarot - Death
Demystifying the Tarot - Temperance
Demystifying the Tarot - The Devil
Demystifying the Tarot - The Tower
Demystifying the Tarot - The Star
Demystifying the Tarot - The Moon
Demystifying the Tarot - The Sun
Demystifying the Tarot - Judgement
Demystifying the Tarot - The World

Desmistificando o Tarot - Os 22 Arcanos Maiores.

Desmistificando O Tarot: O Louco

Desmistificando o Tarot: O Mago

Desmistificando o Tarot: A Papisa

Desmistificando o Tarot: A Imperatriz

Desmistificando o Tarot : O Imperador

Desmistificando o Tarot : O Papa

Desmistificando o Tarot : Os Enamorados

Desmistificando o Tarot : O Carro

Desmistificando o Tarot : A Força

Desmistificando o Tarot: O Eremita

Desmistificando o Tarot - A Roda da Fortuna

Desmistificando O Tarot - A Justiça

Desmistificando O Tarot - O Enforcado

Desmistificando O Tarot - A Morte

Desmistificando o Tarot - A Temperança

Desmistificando o Tarot - O Diabo

Desmistificando o Tarot - A Torre

Desmistificando o Tarot - A Estrela

Desmistificando o Tarot - A Lua

Desmistificando o Tarot - O Sol

Desmistificando o Tarot - O Julgamento

Desmistificando o Tarot - O Mundo

Standalone

Aiming for Success

Raising the standarts of your relationship

Será que é sério

Watch for more at https://linktr.ee/zondradosanjos.

About the Author

Zondra's writing is about helping people to learn and reach their goals and aspirations in life.

In her books, she explores the mysteries of Tarot, spirituality, occult, self-love, relationships, and life itself.

Zondra is a dedicated blogger, author, professional psychic, spiritual advisor, relationship/life coach, and occultist, committed to helping people from all around the world.

Read more at https://linktr.ee/zondradosanjos.

About the Publisher

Thank you so much for taking the time to read one of my books.

Kindly provide a review to enable me to enhance my writing abilities and provide you with more insightful books.